knots

i've never met,
a better version of myself,
until i met you,
you taught me,
more about myself,
than i could ever learn,
on my own.

knots and roses

i'm going to love you,
in all the ways that you need,
love every detail of you,
because you deserve,
an endless unconditional love,
loving you is the only way to live.

knots and roses

revival
you revived my heart, with a love that's real. you pulled off the seal and opened my heart up to you. now, you're more than enough to keep my heart happier than ever before. you always give more, i couldn't be luckier for your existence.

knots and roses

miracle
you'll always stay in my heart because you know me best. you're the best treasure i ever found inside of my chest. and thanks to you, i'm always feeling blessed. you became the miracle that i didn't expect.

knots and roses

i cannot promise you,
a life of perfection,
or the utopia that you dream of,
but i can promise you,
that i will give you,
the very best that life has to offer,
including my heart and soul,
and my unwavering loyalty.

knots and roses

my patience was worth it,
because i found someone perfect,
and it will forever be,
one of my greatest achievements.

knots and roses

i was counting down forever,
until i met you,
now i spend the rest of my life,
together.

knots and roses

i fell in love with you,
as soon as i found myself,
i was lost in your beautiful eyes.

knots and roses

we didn't meet by chance,
it was fate,
it was always meant to be,
our souls met in a different life,
and reunited in this one.

favourite part
life throws twists and turns but you're my favourite part. so, in every chapter i treasure your heart. giving you all my affection. ensuring your soul has my full protection. there's nothing that i would trade for you. and inside my heart, there will always be a place for you. there's no one like you that can make me laugh. and you always keep me on the safest path. you are my favourite part of living. you were the only part i was missing.

knots and roses

eternal
from the bottom of my heart, i'll love you through every storm. when the blizzards find us, i'll keep your heart warm. your struggles will be mine, i'll share every ounce of pain. i'll keep you sheltered from every drop of rain. i'll be your shield and your safety net. i'll extinguish all your regrets. i'll be your comforting shoulder and listening ear. i'll wipe away all your tears. and the well of love in my heart for you, extends infinitely. because i want to be with you through every ounce of happiness and difficulty. i can say with utmost certainty. that my soul was matched with yours for eternity.

knots and roses

i wake up early,
just to watch you sleep peacefully,
the whole world stops because it's just us,
it's just us two and nothing else matters.

knots and roses

when i close my eyes,
it's just you and i,
it's peacefully bright,
and when i open my eyes again,
i see the light your face radiates.

knots and roses

please stay close,
and never leave,
because you've turned into,
all of my memories.

inseparable
i could never let you go. i can't give up the memories we've made and the ones we're going to make. you're in every corner of my mind so it's impossible to take a break from you. i could never let go of your hands, we're in this journey called life, together. our souls are now intertwined forever. i could never let go of you because you mean everything to me. so i hope you smile when you're thinking of me. and when your heart is sinking, i hope it lifts back up with the thought of me. i hope every hug, kiss, and touch, leaves an everlasting warmth in your heart. i hope with me you never let go, knowing that you're loved and celebrated in every way.

knots and roses

i've become addicted,
to everything that involves you,
every word and every action,
i'm addicted to you,
and now i need you,
in every aspect of my life,
to survive.

knots and roses

thanks to you,
i can let go of the past,
and look forward,
to the future.

knots and roses

i've been hurt more times,
than i can remember,
but you've healed me,
so i can forget all of my scars.

knots and roses

you became my moon,
when i needed guidance,
out of what felt like,
eternal darkness.

knots and roses

everywhere and everything
you're in every corner of my mind. every turn that i take, you're always easy to find. ingrained in every layer of my skin. you make sure my world always spins. keeping me grounded and sane. washing away any stains. you're part of every action and thought. you're part of every dream and breath. you're part of me for eternity.

knots and roses

when the grey clouds take over,
when the rain drops,
when lightning strikes,
when the snow falls,
i know you're always there to save me,
you remind me of everything better,
so when the sun shines,
and the skies are blue,
it reminds me of you.

knots and roses

with each day,
i feel more and more,
at peace with you,
calming every storm,
extinguishing every fire,
settling my heart,
in a safe place.

knots and roses

my days felt incomplete,
until you filled them,
with an impossible contentment,
that i never thought existed.

knots and roses

if i met you again,
i'd fall in love,
with you,
again and again,
until this world ends.

knots and roses

i was so lucky to find you,
because you're one in a million stars,
a star that never ends,
a star that shines infinitely.

knots and roses

any other way
you're my other half and i wouldn't have it any other way. because you're always there with the umbrella on rainy days. you complete my sentences when i don't know what to say. and with every storm, you're here to stay. you put my heart at ease, extinguishing my anxiety. and you fight every obstacle defiantly. you're forever doing more than enough. you're fluent in our language of love. i don't know how we could ever be apart. because you know how to heal every fragment of my heart.

knots and roses

just like that
let's fall in love again, like the first time. because i could fall for you forever, like the first time. let's get lost in each other's mind all over again. let's stare into each other's until we lose track of time. because loving you gave me the hope i needed to live. we built a love where we equally give. sharing each other's shoulders when we needed someone to lean on. and just like that, we became each other's safe space.

knots and roses

you're the one thing,
that i can't stand to lose,
because you've become my everything,
you've become my home.

knots and roses

if you ever disappeared,
i'd search for you,
in the deepest crevices,
at the bottom of the ocean,
on top of the highest mountain,
i'd keep on searching for you,
even if i never find you,
i'd never stop looking for you,
because i can't live with you.

knots and roses

i know you can hear me,
when my heart calls out for you,
you always know how i feel,
and you're always here to help me heal.

lean on
you've been my only shoulder to lean on. you became my hero, my miracle, a natural phenomenon. even in silence, you've always heard my cries out for help. you've always found a way to put me before yourself. i'm forever grateful for you being the one person i can fully trust. and now i can't live without your touch. you've healed my heart in places that disappeared. thanks to you, all of the clouds have cleared. you've been my shoulder to lean on, and i will be yours forever.

knots and roses

with you and i,
there's no in between,
we share our hearts and souls,
there's nothing in between.

knots and roses

sometimes i think of you,
i realise that i don't know,
what i would do without you,
because i don't know,
a life without you.

knots and roses

clear
the future has always been clear with you. having you by my side, means there's no fears with you. there's no turbulence because you bring stability. and the storms always disappear because you bring tranquillity. you make the coldest days worthwhile. and on the cloudiest days you bring the brightest smile.

a home

let's build a home together. somewhere our love lasts forever. let's build it from scratch from the floor to the ceiling. a sanctity where we can focus on healing. picking windows that let the right light enter our hearts. the perfect shaped doors where adventures start. we can paint the walls together, so our love is in every coat. we'll put it all together so we can find peace in being remote. building a solid foundation brick by brick. every piece of furniture and decoration will be our pick. we'll plant trees that will grow with our love. and we'll keep building until it's enough. we'll get there, bit by bit, piece by piece. we'll build a home for our souls to find peace.

knots and roses

let's agree to love each other forever,
because i can't see myself with anyone else,
standing by each other's side,
facing adversity together,
battling the wars to be victorious together,
and making the happiest of memories,
memories that can never erased.

knots and roses

before i met you,
love was just a mystery,
now thanks to you,
love will be written,
for the rest of history.

knots and roses

i'm trying to figure out this life,
with you by my side,
because without your support,
i wouldn't make it to the other side.

knots and roses

sometimes i wish,
i could meet you again,
for the first time,
because there's no sweeter feeling,
than falling for you.

knots and roses

what love means
when i think of love, you're the only thing that comes to mind. your beautiful face and your stunning smile, it always leaves me in awe. i wouldn't change anything about the love i have because it revolves around you. when i think of love, i think of the hope and joy you fill my heart with. you give me every part of you, you make it easy to believe in the love we have. the laughter and love you bring is something i've never had. i'm so lucky to have an eternal running stream of love. i can't change the definition of love to fit anything other than you.

knots and roses

don't ever change,
you're perfect in every way,
your laughter is so infectious,
your voice is so harmonic,
your smile is so captivating,
your beauty is so majestic,
your soul is so comforting,
your heart is so loving,
there is nothing i could change,
about you.

knots and roses

you defined love for me,
because of you,
love is more than just a feeling,
it's something so unique,
that words can't describe it.

fool
i would have been a fool for never falling in love with you. because it was meant to be. completing each other's worlds. healing the cracks that have been hidden beneath the surface. you erased the darkness that once overshadowed my existence. falling in love with you was my best decision, even though it came naturally. you changed my life in a way that i never could have imagined.

knots and roses

summers
my best summers have been spent with you. so i know the rest of my life will be content with you. i spent those summers in the greenest fields and bluest skies. i always had the best view in my eyes. staring into your eyes, i knew i met the most perfect person. when i felt your love, i knew my soulmate was certain. listening to you speak, felt like the sweetest symphony. and your presence alone let me feel like i could live this life blissfully.

knots and roses

everything that i do,
i'd only do for you,
because you're worth,
all the effort,
the pressure,
and the stresses of this life.

knots and roses

words can't do justice,
for how much i love you.

knots and roses

when i stare into your eyes,
i see every memory,
and the future,
where our love blooms endlessly.

knots and roses

precious
no one can love me better than you do. because you treat our memories as something so precious. treasuring every moment, capturing every ounce of love in a photograph. cherishing every sunset. preserving every smile. you protect every corner of my heart. and there isn't a single nook and cranny that you forget. you've saved every part of me in a permanent file.

knots and roses

everyone has desires and dreams,
but you've always been mine.

knots and roses

the missing piece
the laws of attraction pulled me into you. i was pulled in by your stunning smile. i was captured by the sparkle in your eyes. and the attraction i felt towards you was impossible to deny. i've never discovered a masterpiece like you. a soul that always makes me feel at peace. and a heart that gives me endless butterflies. i'm stuck on every word that leaves your lips. the sweetest voice that's become embedded in my mind. you're so immaculate and flawless. words aren't enough to describe your perfection. and the moment i fell for you, i didn't need to be cautious. because it's impossible not to feel complete affection. when i met you, i found my other half. the missing piece to complete my puzzle.

knots and roses

soulmates
when they told me about soulmates, they never mentioned someone like you. besides bringing me happiness and life. you find a way to make the stars align. you're always there when i need you the most. you never forget to keep me close. i found my soulmate, someone to match my soul and aura. someone to keep me floating in the water. you take me to the moon and back, exploring everything this universe has to offer.

knots and roses

anyone can love you,
but my love for you,
equates to more than,
every grain of sand,
on this earth.

knots and roses

if i were to ever get lost from you,
i hope i'll be returned to you.

knots and roses

and when i miss you,
i experience a heartache,
that is humanely impossible,
to endure.

the east side
if we ever get separated, meet me on the east side. the place where we first met. the one location i could never forget. i'll find my way back to you all over again. enduring sleet, snow, and rain. tackling every obstacle. journeying through the deepest jungles. tearing down every vine and branch. climbing to every summit, risking any and every avalanche. for you i'll find a way over every broken bridge. and if i had one wish, i would use it on finding you.

knots and roses

attached
i'll never let go as because i know you'll never let go. i'll follow you wherever the wind blows. i'll search the skies for you a thousand times. i'll drive across the roads for you for infinite miles. because the thought of being without you drives me crazy. so i'm not ashamed to admit that i need you daily. you keep me warm in the blistering storms. keeping me afloat during floods, on our own secluded boat. there's nothing to keep us apart. because we'll always share each other's heart.

knots and roses

thank you,
for bringing hope,
back into my heart,
for bringing happiness,
back into my smile,
and for bringing love,
back into my eyes.

knots and roses

i've been lost in your eyes,
in love with you,
since i met you,
mesmerised by your beautiful eyes,
locked into loving you,
for eternity.

knots and roses

when i describe you to other people,
they imagine you with wings,
carrying a crown and a halo,
all at the same time,
as if you're my very own angel.

knots and roses

angelic
she really has become the angel i needed in this world full of demons. saving me from myself and the harshest seasons. drying my eyes when the rain doesn't stop falling. catching me before i slip and start stalling. she's always standing by my side even in the middle of the jungle. even when i crumble, she never lets me stumble. holding every part of me together when i feel at my lowest. she's given me the support i need in every moment. mending and guiding me with every mistake. because of her, the building is the last one standing in every earthquake.

knots and roses

you brought a softness to my heart,
that i never knew existed,
you calmed the storm,
that has been ravaging my soul.

knots and roses

all my life i've been searching,
for the sparkle in your eyes,
hoping i meet the sweetest soul alive,
and to be in the deepest love,
that humanity has never known.

knots and roses

i wish i could spend every day,
and every second of my life,
loving you in every way.

knots and roses

if you were to die,
i would die too,
because there's no me,
without you.

knots and roses

for you,
i would sacrifice,
anything and everything,
just to see you smile.

knots and roses

you saved me,
from the depths of hell,
when my world was burning,
and everything was falling apart,
you saved me from hell.

knots and roses

you pulled me out of the darkness,
and showed me the brighter things in life,
so i'm eternally grateful,
for your presence in my world.

knots and roses

made for you
i'll never find someone that will love me the way you love me. because you understand my love language in every way. filling in the missing pieces. comforting me when i need it the most. encouraging me to be the best version of myself. reassuring me that everything will be okay. it feels like i was made for you.

knots and roses

i'll give you my shoulder to rely on,
a soul that you can lie on,
and a heart to be loved by.

knots and roses

just for you
i'll carry the weight of the world on my shoulders just to make your life easier. i'll emancipate you from the demons that send you meteors. i can't help wanting and needing to protect you. and there's nothing that needs changing to perfect you. loving you comes naturally. i'm so fortunate that i'm able to love you in this galaxy. because discovering you feels like a miracle. and our love just keeps growing as it stays reciprocal.

knots and roses

the pain and suffering,
the heartaches and heartbreaks,
it was all worth it,
because it got me to you,
in the end.

knots and roses

thank you,
for being patient with me,
and loving me,
in the way that i understand,
and for compromising,
where it's needed,
and for being compatible,
in the finest of details.

knots and roses

you saved me from myself,
gave me help when i was helpless,
you taught me to love myself,
showing me how to be selfless,
your love became my cure,
it became my therapy,
i don't think it's wrong to say,
because of you i'm happier this way.

knots and roses

i still get lost in your,
chocolate eyes,
constantly reminding me,
of some of my favourite things,
cinnamon, coffee, and caramel,
and every part of you.

knots and roses

a minute without you feels wasted,
and every second with you is precious,
time is so short,
and time is so valuable,
but time with you is priceless.

knots and roses

sparks
before meeting you, i gave up on the idea of love. i experienced so much in life that i finally had enough. but sparks flew when our eyes locked in. and the love birds dropped in. my heart was filled with hope and comfort. and the affection was more than just abundant. you made this black and white world colourful. painting a future that looked wonderful. thanks to you, i changed my perspective on dreaming. you taught me that dreams can be redeeming. that all my dreams can come true. so i'll always be thanking you.

knots and roses

you gave me hope,
that love lasts forever.

knots and roses

every time i look up,
at the night sky,
searching for the brightest star,
i end up finding you every time,
and it reminds me how,
you're one in a million.

knots and roses

it felt like,
i was soul searching forever,
until i met you,
and everything fell into place.

knots and roses

i've never found someone so special,
you're someone that you can only find,
once in a lifetime.

marry me
marry me, not just for now but forever and any other lifetime. so, i can show you that for you, there's no mountain i wouldn't climb. marry me, and i'll give you comfort and protection. we'll plant seeds in the dirt and build an unbreakable connection. i'll chase the stars for you, just so you can smile. for you, i'll travel infinite miles. dedicating myself to loving you in the way that you deserve. healing you from all the memories that hurt. and your true self doesn't need to stay hidden. marry me, because our love was written. from this end of the universe, to the end of time. the love that we share is more than a sign. it's a miracle that we both needed. a piece of paradise is all that we needed.

knots and roses

i've dreamt of a future with you,
planning out every year,
what our summers would look like,
the home that we'd build,
i'm so thankful you're living this future,
with me.

knots and roses

i promise,
i won't just love you for the moment,
i'll love you for an entire lifetime.

knots and roses

please love me,
please never stop loving me,
in this life and the next,
love me endlessly for,
the rest of forever.

knots and roses

when your tears fall,
mine fall too,
because our love,
shares everything.

knots and roses

i want you to stay,
by my side,
until the end of time.

knots and roses

the memories we've collected,
has made me look forward,
to a future with you.

unstoppable

i can't stop loving you. because we made the sweetest memories. drifting through the bluest oceans, fascinated by most extraordinary marine life. sinking into the sand at every beach. staring at the silky skies, cloud watching for hours. finding the greenest fields to enjoy the peace we found in each other. we bring a special type of happiness to our lives that can't be found anywhere else. we erase the negativity that comes with every grey cloud. sheltering each other from the rain that brings us down. it's no surprise that i can't stop loving you.

knots and roses

words can't explain the love,
that i feel for you,
a thousand pictures,
couldn't show you either,
because this love runs deeper,
than any other love that i've known.

knots and roses

i know that,
no matter what trials,
and tribulations i face,
i can survive them,
with you by my side.

better
if you ever need me, i'll give you myself unconditionally. i'll complete favours for you infinitely. i won't hesitate to lay down my heart and soul for you. i'll give up pieces of myself to keep you whole. i couldn't imagine loving you any less. so i'm more than happy to take on all of your troubles and stress. i'll dedicate myself to you forever. because you made this world so much better.

knots and roses

loving you forever,
is a promise,
that i could never break.

knots and roses

i wish i could tell you why,
but words can't explain,
that i keep falling in love with you,
and i hope that never ends.

knots and roses

you are the sweetest love,
that i have ever known,
nothing could replace you,
you are a piece of love itself.

only one
you're my only one. you're everything my heart desires. you're everything my soul needs. you keep the flames alive. and you keep the engine running. you're the only one that i could ever be with for the rest of eternity. it's hard to tell you that i love you in a million different ways, but i made a start with this one. you're my best friend, my partner, and my soulmate. you are everything that i can't explain. you're my only one, for now and forever, no one else could replace you.

knots and roses

i wish that i could spend,
every moment with you,
i know that it's unrealistic,
but i hope i'll spend,
my final moments with you.

knots and roses

one of the best things,
i've ever done,
is fall in love with you.

knots and roses

victorious
i wasn't done explaining what love really means. because it's made up of so many different chapters and scenes. intricate details that bring perfect chemistry. it brings feelings that feel heavenly. love includes patience and slow days. there's no solid formula to make the love stay. everyone has their own picture to paint. sometimes that needs understanding and restraint. thinking about someone else before thinking about yourself. because ultimately, together you're building a unique type of wealth. it's hard to explain love in words, sometimes it requires actions and time. and you never face the mountains alone, it's always a united climb. the puzzle falls into place when you see the world as one. and when you feel that in love, it feels like you've truly won.

knots and roses

she is every wish,
that i ever wanted.

knots and roses

she got rid of my nightmares,
and made my dreams come true.

love is so much more
love isn't just about all the fun parts. it's more than just love. it includes building a foundation and bringing warm emotions to each other's heart. love also means sticking by each other's side through the storms. being a listening ear on the rough days. being a shoulder to cry on. being someone to rely on. sometimes it's about the little things. sometimes love isn't pretty, sometimes it's the most beautiful thing you can think about. love should bring you peace. it should be a safe space. love should bring a genuine smile to your face. love isn't the same for everyone, we mould it to what works best. there are so many aspects to love that we misunderstand, so it's important to find that right person who understands you, just make sure you understand them. because i found that person in you.

knots and roses

all my problems,
feel so little,
once you're in the picture.

knots and roses

you're the only place,
i could ever feel,
complete peace.

knots and roses

thank you for letting me into your mind,
thank you for letting me help you heal,
i'm grateful for being able to understand you,
you let me into your world to stay,
and now we've built a home together.

knots and roses

you can show me all your flaws,
share all your insecurities,
i promise i'll love you all the same.

knots and roses

you gave me a safe space,
a place where i can be vulnerable,
and a chance to be comfortable.

knots and roses

your eyes hold memories,
that are one of a kind,
holding a happiness within,
that makes them sparkle.

knots and roses

one of a kind
when they ask me why i love you, i tell them about your perfection. and how we have this one of a kind connection. i mention how you're beautiful in infinite ways that words can't explain, and picture aren't enough. and the feelings i feel are more than just love. you possess a beauty that's so magnificent, that my eyes aren't worthy. and beneath the surface, you're always trying to protect me from things that could hurt me. a character that's sweeter and kinder than any other soul i've met. you're someone that no one could ever forget. your smile lights up worlds instead of rooms. you bring peace and blessings when the skies are filled with gloom.

knots and roses

i've been let down,
so many times before,
but you never disappoint,
you never give up on me,
you always support me to the fullest.

knots and roses

i just want to be,
my best possible self,
for myself and for you,
i want to do anything i can,
to help,
because that love,
keeps me going.

knots and roses

when i close my eyes,
you're always there,
comforting me in the darkness,
loving me in the toughest of times,
you feel like a breath of heaven.

the red-string theory
we were always meant to be together. our souls were destined forever. connected by a red string, it was only a matter of time until we met. our fate was already set. that's why our connection is undeniably meant to be. one way or another, our love was meant to be. we're the right people for each other to be the best versions of ourselves. any path that we took, was bound to lead back to one another. we are each other's final destination. the universe was always pulling us back to each other for eternity. you're at the end of branch and at the top of every mountain. it's impossible to recreate a life without you. because we complete each other in ways that others can't imagine. elevating and healing together, it wouldn't work any other way.

knots and roses

i hope this love with you,
can be endless,
because without you,
i feel restless.

knots and roses

despite our love being so strong,
i still get scared of losing you,
because you're my weakness in this world,
and you're the last thing i would want to lose.

knots and roses

you gave me hope,
when i thought it ran out,
you brought me back to life,
when i had nothing left,
thanks to you,
i believe in hope again.

knots and roses

i'm happiest in your company,
because there's no place,
like home.

knots and roses

i wouldn't be able find someone like you,
not even in a million lifetimes.

knots and roses

the honeymoon phase
they said it's just the 'honeymoon phase', and that it won't last. looking back at it together, we both laughed. because a decade has almost passed, and the love only ever grew. we've stuck together like glue. attached to each other from the depths of our hearts. our souls intertwined to the point they can never grow apart. this love was never a phase, it was a permanent declaration. our eyes never stopped locking in with complete admiration. this is more than just love, this is extraordinarily euphoric.

knots and roses

i hope the smile on your face,
stays permanently,
because it's one of the most,
beautiful things that exist.

knots and roses

others think i'm crazy,
for my love being obsessive,
but is it wrong,
to say i can't get enough of you.

knots and roses

i appreciate that i can depend on you,
someone who loves me unconditionally,
that's all i could ever ask for.

knots and roses

perpetual
it was foolish to think that i would only feel happiness when i fell in love with you. that isn't normal, happiness isn't a permanent feeling. but your love is perpetual regardless of any situation that is thrown our way. but whenever i feel sadness, you know how to erase the misery. destroying my anxiousness, reminding me of the happiness in my history. protecting me when i don't know how. reassuring me by diminishing all of my doubts. thanks to you, i'm able to appreciate happiness properly. and the best happiness i discovered was the one that we created perfectly.

knots and roses

you are the only rose,
that i need in a field,
of endless flowers.

knots and roses

thank you,
for believing in me enough,
for supporting me in my dreams,
for having faith in me,
especially when i didn't,
you're my most precious asset.

anniversary
it's our anniversary, and i'm already looking forward to the next one. because the day i met you, was the day i felt complete. my soul searching came to an end. because i found my eternal companion and my best friend, all in one person. it was meant to be, so we were always destined to meet. i met you on a friday and married you on a sunday. it wasn't overnight but it felt like it was only yesterday. i'm sure our love existed before we did. because everyone tells us we're a perfect fit. and i couldn't agree more, as nothing else fills me with so much life. thank you for being more than just my wife. i hope these words remind you, that i always think of you.

knots and roses

when i'm with you,
i always end up on the moon,
in a whole different dimension,
where time and space stand still,
and it's just you and i.

knots and roses

she's there whenever i look up at the sky,
she's there when i look at any star,
she's there when the lights go out,
and everything ceases to exist.

knots and roses

you're in all of my dreams,
and you're there when i wake up,
you're in every thought,
you can never escape my mind,
because you're one of a kind.

knots and roses

you're the one chapter,
that i hope would never end.

Printed in Great Britain
by Amazon